Quote from Jimmy Page, Led Zeppelin

# Word of mouth

"Printed by 1010 Printing International Limited through
Print Vision."

Published in 2012 by:
Bill Milne Studio
121 west 19th street
New York N.Y. 10011 USA
ISBN 978-0-9838504-9-6
"Printed in China"
10 9 8 7 6 5 4 3 2 1
First Printing

# TABLE OF CONTENTS

Market Lane Coffee

Everyone has a story. I would like to share mine, in order to give you perspective on how I came to fall in love with food and the people that I call my friends especially one in particular, Chef Grant MacPherson.

I grew up in a small village, further north than most would care to inhabit. My family was working class. Growing up, our evening ritual revolved around the family meal. My father provided a modest lifestyle for us, yet every night he would come home from work and within the hour we would be seated around a veritable feast. My mother prepared our meals on a small stove with a single pot which they purchased when first married. We knew not how food came to our table - Just that it did, and that it brought us together. We shared this time talking about life. Love and affection came from these times. I barely experienced a meal away from the family table until I was 18 years old, when I left my childhood home to pursue my education… And the world opened before my eyes in ways I could never have imagined. It's how I met my wife, it defines the language we speak and how we interact everyday.

Food was so VISUAL. It became suddenly exciting and magical, the ambition became a career. I wanted to light dishes to accent their character. I met chefs from around the world, tasted cuisine from every continent and ate in the finest restaurants. Even to this day, the experiences seem dreamlike.
Grant saw that I want to showcase his food, that I understood how he plates a dish and was willing and able capture the passion he brings to the overall experience of eating.

Grant is like my twin brother and if we looked more alike I would almost believe it to be so. We can literally finish each other sentences - Assuming we don't lose our thoughts to laughter first. We have traveled and tasted the world together. A special, shared bond means that creatively, we understand what is trying to be achieved almost without words and it has been a special privilege to have worked together on this project. Grant's passion and talent shines through every dish on every page.

Please enjoy Word of Mouth
Bill Milne

Bill Milne

Fish Slice

# GRANT MacPHERSON

I am a Chef. I love food. Ingredients are everything
and quality is the key to good cooking.  I try to live
my life like a recipe… Work with seasonal ingredients,
prepare a scrupulous mise en place, execute the method
meticulously and season correctly.

I was born in Dundee, Scotland, before our family
migrated to Johannesburg, South Africa and then to
Alberta, Canada.  My adult life has sustained this
theme of relocation - I've never been one to stay too
long in the same place. During these early years, I had
very little interest in food, although my Mother was an
extraordinary homemaker and had mastered the British
classics such as Sunday roasts, shepherd's pie, corned
beef and fruit trifle. Memories of school are
unpleasant... It's never fashionable to have an accent
when you're a child, so to combat the inevitable
bullying I worked on developing my communication
skills, learning how to quickly connect with people
and overcome barriers- A trait which has served me well
throughout life.

In 1978 my culinary career began insalubriously (as
they generally do), at the bottom of an endless pile of
chicken wings in a St. Catherine's, Ontario restaurant
named 'Bugsy's'.  The house specialty were real
Buffalo Wings, so every weekend was spent chopping and
bagging 1000s of pounds of cold, clammy chicken - But I
didn't care, I was earning my keep and paying my way.
Yes, I was missing out on 'normal' teenage social
opportunities, but that was a sacrifice I was willing
to make in order to eventually earn the right to wear
one of those white jackets and cook. By the time I was
promoted to dish-washer, it was all over... I had
fallen completely and utterly in love with the Kitchen.

In 1980 and thanks to the generous guidance of Beacon
Motor Inn's Chef Darrell Firby, my Cook's
Apprenticeship was underway. I had met a best friend in
Bus-boy and pizza maker Rick Buerger, and in the great
industry tradition upheld by Hospitality workers around
the globe, we discovered the party lifestyle.  I won't
go into the details because you've no doubt heard it
all before - Industry Standard is that chefs will work
hard and play even harder. All I'll say is that, Rick
and I blazed and boozed our way through those years
with red-eyed gusto, to a classic soundtrack of Black
Sabbath, ZZ-Top, Ted Nugent, The Who and Kiss.  Good
times. Then it was time to grow up.  Things became a
little more serious than chicken wings...

JEAN-LOUIS
COOKING WITH THE SEASONS

Chef Jean-Louis Palladin

I should say right now, I've been incredibly lucky to have been influenced by so many incredible mentors, from the very beginning of my career - I still smile fondly when I remember turning vegetables with the late Norbert Chabot and laugh out loud when I think about the brilliant  Mr. Rudy Mack at Four Seasons Toronto, my springboard and safety net hotel brand, either side of and during a London apprenticeship. It was while working my third Four Seasons property, this time in Vancouver, when I met friend, Kim Canteenwalla and Chef Bernard Ibarra.

I dreamed of Australia, the big island with the gorgeous beaches and endless rivers of Victoria Bitter. My dreams became reality when I went to work at Kables Restaurant at the Regent Hotel in Sydney with the Chef's Chef - Serge Dansereau. Serge is without doubt, one of the most significant influences on my career. He is a culinary pioneer. Under Serge's command, Kables was the first ever hotel restaurant in Australia to win 3 hats. It's thanks to this man, I discovered the unparalleled quality of specialist Australian produce. Under his guidance I left behind the typical traits of a young lad (beer & girls) and found myself in a willing state of complete focus.

I eventually left Australia for Kuala Lumpur, Malaysia to be part of the opening of the Regent Hotel as Grill Chef and it was here I discovered the United Nations of Food and Beverage! Asian line staff, French and Swiss, Spanish and American Hotel Managers… And one Canadian Chef with a bumblebee accent, fresh off the boat from Australia with my treasured stash of cassette tapes. Just like the UN, there were hierarchies and hissy fits.  I toughened up and learned from some incredible characters, then jetted off to Hawaii and the Ritz Carlton, where I first met the Trio of Excellence… MPS Puri, Phillippe Padovani and Ian Michael Coughlan.

One more stop, Chef De Cuisine at the Pierre Cardin-owned Maxims de Paris, The Regent in Singapore. Swiss Chef, Bruno Von Siebenthal was the Big Boss… But before I find myself reminiscing about 1993 and accepting a position at the illustrious Raffles Hotel, it's here I will pause because according to my vision for this book - We've now reached Chapter One. Rather than be defined by ingredients or courses, this book will be segmented by Venues.  You'll be taken on a journey through the most succulent slices of my culinary career; you'll meet characters of influence and read recipes which define the culture, the time and the place. Please try very hard to stop yourself from
licking the pages, which are bursting with visual flavor courtesy of photographer genius, Bill Milne.

This is my walkabout,
Grant MacPherson

FaMILY ⊛

THaNK YOU

PaRENTs
Ian aNd Dorothy MacPherson
LiFE PaRTNER
Cheryl MacPherson
sONs, Graeme aNd Connor
SISTER aNd HUSBaND
Lisa aNd John Searles
sONs, Ian aNd Jacob

Graeme

Connor

1010 printing

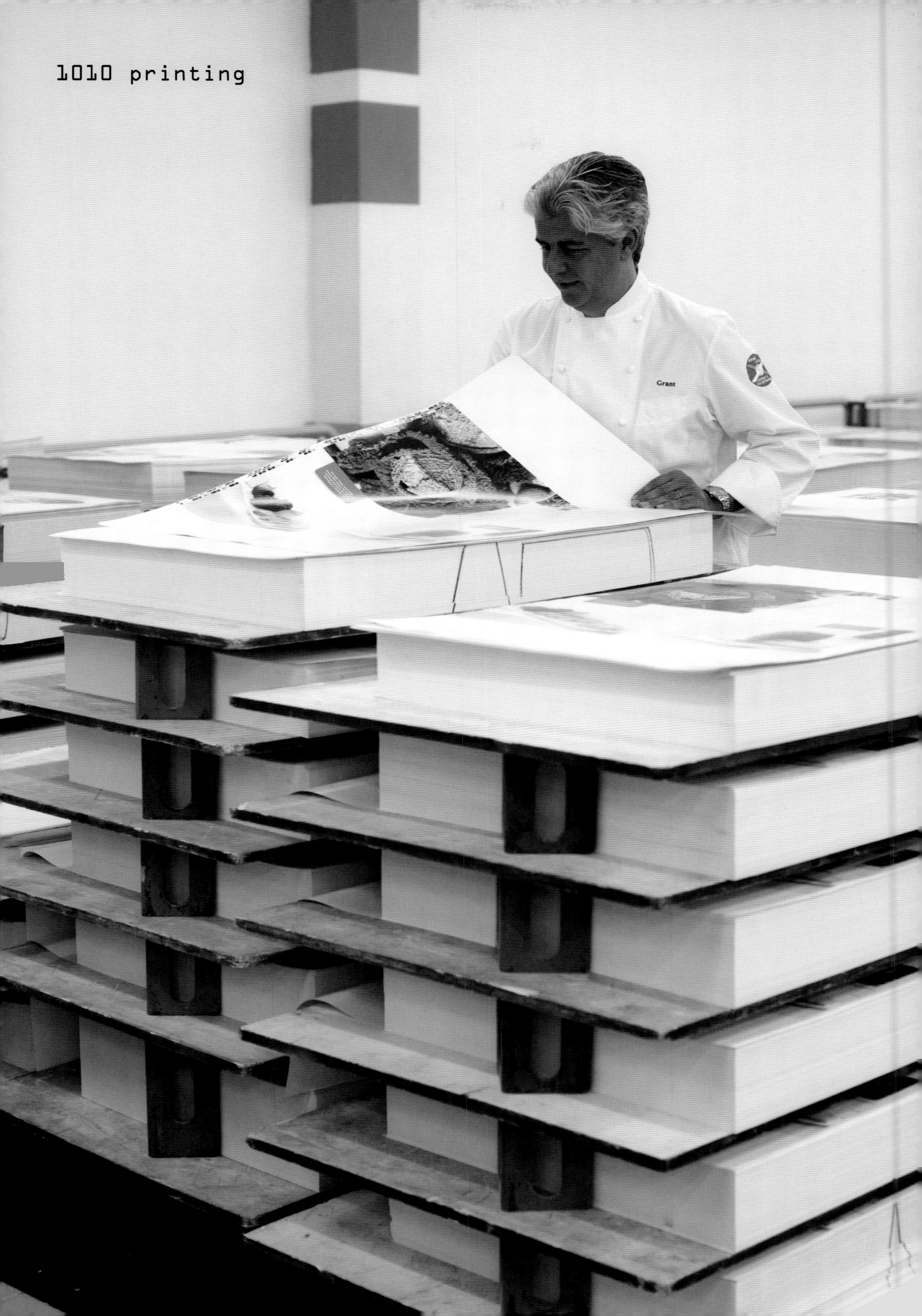

# Game Change

The game has changed. Our Industry is on fast forward, inextricably linked with a media juggernaut cultivating consumer obsession with produce, technology, appliances, techniques and personalities. Western society's inexhaustible craving for food culture has brought commercial cooking into the home kitchen and the family now speaks Chef as a second language.

In night-time suburbia, the call to arms of "Dinner's ready!" is long gone... You're much more likely to hear "C'mon kids, I'm plating up!" Next to the food processor you'll find a domestic-sized cryovac machine, blast-chiller and sous vide bath. Meat'n'3veg is now a grass-fed wet-aged steak in a natural jus with a celeriac puree. But best of all, bookshelves across the globe are groaning under the weight of a covetable cook book food porn library and I have to say, this can't be a bad thing!

I can't put my knife on the time when this food culture obsession began... Was it a slow trickle or a torrent I missed because I was drowning in a project and paddling too hard to notice? Charles Darwin said "It's not the strongest of the species that survives, nor the most intelligent - It is the one most adaptable to change." and I agree. However (and you knew there'd be a 'however') I don't always agree with the tinkering of food genetics. I'm not thrilled about the development of advanced kitchen appliances which delete vital steps within a recipe, dumbing-down technique and ultimately of course, flavour.

It's amusing to me, that Joe/Anne Bloggs can become a brand name chef in just 16 thrilling 45 minute episodes... "It's been an incredible journey!" The positive side of the reality cooking show phenomenon, is that the exposure and industry interface expands and educates the public palate - Hopefully giving an insight into what we professional Cooks do for the love and a living. I think, where cooking is involved, time & technique go hand-in-hand. Learning obsessively however, can cause claustrophobia and that's when you need to make room for innovation.

PEOPLE WHO KNOW THE GAME, CREATED IT AND CHANGED IT

## Industry Influencers

DeRuyter Butler • Bill Milne • Todd Nisbet
Mark Stech-Novak • MPS Puri
Alburn William ª Michael Winner

0
1
4

# 8

Despite living my time thus far in a constant state of inspiration there has always been one consistency of influence an ingredient of powerful and existential proportion… (Nope, not a person and not a deity.) The number 8, the ancient symbol for infinity has been a tap on the shoulder, a green flag and an exclamation mark punctuating my life and career since the day of my birth – 8th August, 1962. Everywhere I look and everything I do is wrapped up in 8's to an almost freaky proportion. It may seem trivial to some but when it's this consistent, you take notice and take some sense of security that you are on track. 8 is the Chinese numeral for luck and prosperity and the Hindu figure for wealth and abundance. It's a magical number for mathematics, physics and the hierarchical levels of identified consciousness. Hmmmm… If we're counting and cooking: 8 bytes make a bit, there are 8 pints to a gallon and 8 pinches in a teaspoon. The opening ceremony of the Summer Olympics in Beijing started at 8 seconds and 8 minutes past 8pm on 8th August 2008. How can Fibonacci, Timothy Leary and 1.2 billion Chinese be wrong?

## DOUBLE CAT

I am a Leo and a Chinese Tiger. A double cat littered in the luck of the number 8. I lunge at opportunity, lap up life and smile with Cheshire satisfaction. I always felt an innate ferocity for food blazing through life with feline tenacity. I take my tiger with me everywhere I go, a reminder to stay strong during the bad days, to maintain balance during the crazy and to appreciate great when it steps up to the plate.

018

# EARNING MY STRIPES ❂
# BLOOD, SWEAT AND SEARS

How can 18 years feel like 18 minutes?

It's been almost 20 years years since this young
Scotsman took determined steps from Canada, lead by my
internal compass spinning me across continents and
still counting.

I'm grateful and proud to look back over a massive
career but at the same time I feel like it is still
just beginning...

I catch myself in contemplation, staring into
reminiscence, rubbing my hand across my chin - I'm
going cross-eyed here!  Looking back, researching my
life for stories to engage and justly illustrate my
career so far...

Yet from a lifetime of habit, my eyes eternally
skittering forward to meet and greet those challenges
ahead.

"Grant MacPherson is one of the world's great chefs.
Period!  Not only is his cuisine infinitely creative,
but in his heart beats the soul of rock and roll -
spirited, multi-flavored music that infuses his dishes,
his menus and his restaurants.  Grant is also one of
the most gracious, generous, talented and energetic men
I've had the pleasure of meeting along the long road of
life.  It's an honor to call him a friend."  -

# BARON WOLMAN, Santa Fe
Rolling Stone's first chief photographer

"I brought Grant from Canada in 1988 to take charge of
the restaurant kitchen at The Regent, Sydney where I was
executive chef. He was young, talented and energetic.
He helped me developed the menus to a point where we
achieved the highest rating of any restaurant in
Australia.

The years I spent with Grant were exciting and rewarding
but one needs to be challenged with new opportunities.
I organised for Grant to take a position at The Regent,
Singapore that eventually lead to taking the very
coveted role of Executive Chef at the world famous
Raffles Hotel. Then he was approached to lead the
kitchens at the Bellagio in Las Vegas demonstrating his
impeccable culinary and human abilities."

SERGE DANSEREAU
Chef / Owner
The Bathers' Pavillion
Balmoral Beach NSW

Red Octopus

"In an age of fatiguing celebrity chefdom, Grant
MacPherson is the real deal ..
An inspirer, innovator and perfectionist .. he leads
from the front with a pan in his hand ..
A culinary democrat .. as comfortable with 'Mee Goreng'
as he is 'Tournedos Rossini'..
A 'General Patton' in chefs whites ... Rock on Grant !"

IAN M. COUGHLAN

President- wynn macau

Writing a C OOK B OOK which is more story
than recipe, and sometimes sounding more fiction than
fact, has forced me to pause a moment and take stock
of the ride.

Treasured memories of tumultuous times, golden
opportunities and unimaginable experiences all riveted
to the fabric of my life by characters, friends and
mentors of platinum grade.

I recall some days almost destroyed me.
Remembering angled lights and colours, I feel the heat
and pressure and I remember the flavours, every single
one of them.

I'm astounded at what can be achieved when you love
something so much that you can work for days, even
months without a rest.
You will sear your flesh to the bone and wear down the
discs in your back like the soft tyre tread of an
ethanol-burning race car.

Like a raging addiction, the kitchen gave me
everything, every day.  Some may say it also took
away.  Let them.
Even at the brink of exhaustion, the chance to rest
would resemble a restraint when all I wanted was to
return to the kitchen to roll out the new idea in my
mind...

"CUL I N A R Y talent is a gift, and Grant is
blessed to have it !!  I have known Grant for over two
decades, had the opportunity to work with him more than
once, and always admired his abilities."

MPS PUR I - Chief Executive Officer of Nira
Hotels

These pages will take you on a tour through some of the biggest destination dining spots in the world.
I am so damn proud to have been a part of them all, an integral part of a venue, the vision and it's kitchen -
There's nothing sweeter than the memory of a team working as one tight unit...

Worshipping at the altar - Those times when you just feel that Kali's in the House.

I may not be able to list all the names, the nights and the nuances but if you were part of the team during these times, at these venues, then I hope you cherished cooking these dishes as much as I did and I still do.
To the wheels that fell off, I hope you found your road and are on track to a destiny of great achievement.

This is a salute to the people who helped me deliver these dreams, as much as it an acknowledgment of the visionaries behind the venues that housed all this grand hospitality.
This job is truly about the indescribable Zen state of a well-oiled machine that is a team sharing one vision with 100% commitment.

All this is part of the memory, I wish to include it all and exclude nothing.

Hope you enjoy my ride via the VENUES that shaped me.

"Every man dies, not every man really lives."
WILLIAM WALLACE

Chef Grey Kunz

The MENTORS,

the team and on the view from both sides of the pass:

Is there a hidden culinary chromosome buried deep in a person's DNA? I often wonder, because this role I love of the Chef is in my bones, it pumps my blood and it fills my lungs. Finding a balance of mental and physical predisposition allows you to become utterly consumed, whereby even the most mundane task is a divine part of the art. Perhaps to the detriment of other areas of my life, I surrendered to the call and found my true purpose. While it's certainly no Sainthood and I'm not curing Cancer, I believe truly great cooking to be a noble art - It's an expression of generosity, a gift of creativity engaging all five senses to elicit a response, generally underpinned by pleasure. Some have a HUNGER for power; others are DRIVEN by dollars. While I'll not deny the advantages of either, at the core I still just want to plate up magic for many. I make my food with love and more importantly, I make it with LIFE.

Beyond the recipe, the method and the mystique I see my team. They are my family and my army. We stand shoulder-to-shoulder, blazing through dockets and our motivation is a mantra of the hive mind, one thought 'Perfectio Pertinaciae'. Some of the Chefs I worked with were idols to me. There would be a sense of awe and inspiration but never intimidation, through which I learned the invaluable rule of working with a team - Give them ownership of task, credit where due and encouragement when eager. Within this book I have listed certain people who have impacted my journey so far. Perhaps they would never have known the intensity of their influence, had it not been for their name in these pages. I can only hope that one day I too will be responsible for inspiration of a similar subversive magnitude…

To Serge Dansereau at The Regent in Sydney, Australia 'Collecting me from Sydney's International airport on my first day in Australia is a gesture I will never forget. The experience that followed simply grew in graciousness and showcased your greatness'.

Life Mentors- portraits
Steve Wynn - Vision
Jimmy Page - passion
Chef Joel Robuchon MOF - perfection
Sirio Maccioni - service
Serge Dansereau - product

# SINGAPORE 093
## RAFFLES HOTEL

Raffles holds a special place in my heart. More legend than hotel, mere mention of its name conjures an image of mythical literary debauchery - Somerset Maugham and Charlie Chaplin wasted on Singapore Slings, tigers shot under billiard tables with the bullets ricocheting off tiffin curry luncheons and high tea silverware. What a place! You can't manufacture that kind of history and style… I realized it's a magnetic combination for the rich and famous as I watched with wonder, the likes of Elizabeth Taylor, Michael Jackson and Jimmy Stewart enjoying my food. Looking back, I'm humbled to realize that my story is somehow woven into the fabric of this Grand Old Lady's colonial hotel petticoats.

Two years working at Raffles for Chef Peter Knipp as Executive Sous Chef sent me on a learning curve so sharp I feel the slices still today. Peter is quintessentially German: Mercedes perfection with a Wusthof edge. This is where I learned The Rules of The Recipes. This is where I first witnessed the power of the Holy Trinity: Cuisine, Service & Environment. This was serious Food & Beverage.

The other key individual during my time at Raffles was Mr MPS Puri, a food and beverage technician and an opposite personality to Knipp. I was sometimes the foil between them learning from their polar perspectives and often witness to some heated moments. Knipp would regularly say he "ate food and beverage managers for breakfast" until he met Puri and experienced his excellence. Always heated but both heroes in their own right.

Thanks to MPS Puri, concepts like The Raffles Cooking Academy and Doc Cheng's trans-Asian restaurant were born. The highlight though was The Raffles' Guest Chef program with a call sheet that read like the Michelin Guide Index - Joel Robuchon MOF, Jean-Louis Palladin, Raymond Blanc, Alain Ducasse... With mentors like that and a team who were united by vision and motivated by perfection, it's no wonder that by the time I left Raffles in '95, I was armed with the techniques, organisation and logistical skills to set me up for a lifetime.

To MPS Puri
"Puri, I have met many influential people but you have truly stuck with me on multiple levels by your innate ability to provide memorable experiences for your guests."

# Singapore Chili Crab

Yield: 2 servings
1 large Dungeness crab
1 tablespoon or 15 ml peanut oil
1 tablespoon or 8 g chopped ginger
2 garlic cloves, finely chopped
1 red Thai chile, halved, seeded and minced
1 cup or 250 ml fish stock
1/4 cup or 50 ml Chinese cooking wine or dry
sherry
1/4 cup or 50 ml tomato sauce
Salt, to taste
1 scallion, cut into 1 inch or 2.5 cm pieces
Cilantro leaves, for garnish
Method:
Using your fingers, pull off large top shell of
crab.
(Reserve shell for garnish.) Turn crab over, and
remove triangular
piece of shell. Remove gills and other unwanted
parts of crab.
Rinse crab well. Chop off claws; crack with a
nutcracker.
Chop remaining crab into quarters.
In large wok or deep skillet over medium-heat,
warm oil.
Add ginger, garlic and chile, and cook 5 seconds;
add crab. Cook 3 minutes. Add fish stock, wine,
tomato sauce and salt; over high heat, bring to
boiling.
Reduce heat to low; simmer 8 to 10 minutes or
until
crab is cooked, stirring occasionally.
During last 2 minutes, stir in scallion.
Presentation:
Garnish with cilantro leaves and crab shell.

"Grant is not only one of my dearest friends but also one of the most respected and talented chef's in the industry"
CHEF HUBERT KELLER, Burger Bar, Fleur, Fleur de Lys - Las Vegas and San Francisco

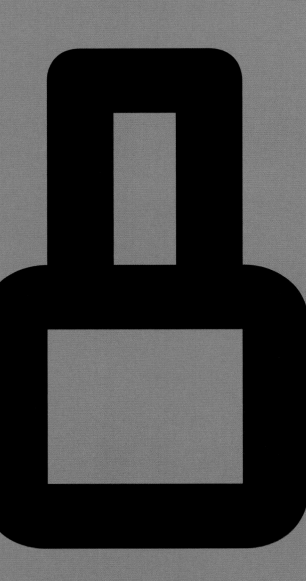

# Eight-Hour Golden Pineapple,

Vanilla Beans,
Inniskillin Ice Wine
Yield: 4 servings
Pineapple:
1 whole ripe golden pineapple
2 cups or 450 g butter
2 cups or 400 g granulated sugar
4 vanilla beans
Garnish:
Vanilla Ice Cream
Mint leaves
Inniskillin ice wine, chilled
Method:
Preheat oven to 200°F/105°C.
Remove skin and eyes from pineapple.
In small saucepan over medium heat, melt butter.
Stir in sugar; cook just until sugar is
dissolved,
stirring constantly. Scrape seeds from vanilla beans;
add to sugar mixture.
Reserve vanilla beans for garnish later.
Place pineapple in baking dish; top with sugar mixture.
Cook 8 hours or until pineapple is golden,
turning occasionally.
Presentation:
Place pineapple on serving platter,
or quarter and serve on 4 plates.
Garnish with ice cream, vanilla beans and mint.
Serve with Inniskillin ice wine.
'

'

# Whole Snapper, "Cantonese-Style"

Yield: 4 servings
1 whole red snapper, 4 to 5 pounds or 1.8 to 2.2 kilos, scaled and cleaned
3 baby bok choy or other Chinese greens, halved lengthwise
1 leek, cut into julienne strips
1 small piece ginger, cut into julienne strips
1/4 cup or 9 g cilantro leaves
1/4 cup or 50 ml soy sauce
1/2 cup or 125 ml peanut oil
Steamed white rice
Method:
Preheat oven to 375°F/190°C. On each side of fish,
make 3 diagonal cuts, about 1/2-inch/1.25 cm deep.
Place bok choy on rack in broiler pan.
Top with red snapper. Bake 18 minutes, or until fish flakes
easily when tested with a fork.
Remove fish from oven; top with leek, ginger and cilantro.
Pour soy sauce over fish.
Presentation:
In small saucepan over medium heat, warm peanut oil.
pour oil over fish, and serve immediately with steamed rice.
'

To Mr. Terence Chew
"Our experience together in the 1992 Frankfurt
Olympics, 42 hours with no sleep, lets have
another German beer".

046

8

# Asian Peanut Brittle

Yield: 1 pound/450 grams
Butter, for pan
1 cup or 200 g granulated sugar
1/4 cup or 50 ml water
1 1/2 cups or 250 g shelled raw peanuts
2 tablespoons or 28 g butter
1 teaspoon or 5 g baking soda
Method:
Butter large cookie sheet. In heavy saucepan
over medium heat, bring sugar and water to a
boil,
stirring constantly until sugar is completely
dissolved. Stir in peanuts.
Set candy thermometer in place, and continue
cooking, stirring frequently,
until temperature reaches 290°F/145°C, or hard-
crack stage (when a small amount of mixture
dropped into very cold water separates into hard
and brittle threads), about 20 minutes.
Remove saucepan from heat; stir in butter and
baking soda; immediately pour onto cookie sheet,
spreading with spatula. Cool completely until
firm.
Presentation:
Break peanut brittle into pieces. Stack on
plate. Store in tightly covered container.
'

Baker Tan
-golden hands

Heirloom tomato salad

# MALAYSIA / 095 - DATAI HOTEL

Perched atop the Northwestern tip of Langkawi Island Malaysia and nestled in rainforest surrounded by the Adaman Sea, Datai Hotel's relatively new fit out was the perfect antithesis to Raffles' tradition-filled edifice. Mr. Jamie Case recruited his dream team and presented us with a deluxe resort calling for a broom and a heavy hand to be pushed through it. We tore it apart. We busted up the original idea and started again, adding layers and layers of quality. We were inexperienced but we knew that we needed a set-up smart enough to continue to build the global reputation Datai deserved. We did it too.

Produce-wise, Datai was heaven on a hook! The location meant access to crazy-fresh fish which we happily loaded with freestyle spices. Malaysians have such a passion for food, but rules were meant to be bent if not broken. We married traditional ingredients with virgin techniques and while local religion forbade the consumption of alcohol and pig… I never intended to offend, but I just couldn't accept a menu bereft of wine however pork was just not an option.

To Alain Ducasse
"Understanding how you built flavours upon a dish still sticks in my mind today. You bought a new level of cuisine to The Raffles Grill."

Jamie was always riding me about food costs. He was the master of the margin and he taught me a lot, but I'll never forget his face when I handed him a fake invoice for $45k worth of white truffles. Then ran. This was a team of up-and-comers, imaginations were running as wild as the landscape around us - It was a great time to teach, and to learn.

Thanks to my earlier stint in Australia, I became secretly addicted to some of the signature products from the great island. Around this time we were the first to start importing these Aussie gifts such as purple Coffin Bay scallops which are now impossible to find, Gippsland lamb and King Island dairy products which seems to be doing a cracking trade these days. These local delicacies can be taken for granted after residing in a place like Australia but they're sorely missed when you realize how spoilt you have been. Take freshly squeezed orange juice as an example.. Doesn't seem a big ask but in Malaysia, it just wasn't on the menu. I couldn't live without it so I had some squeezed, bottled and brought to me - Thus began quite the rendezvous with Redgum who saved my cravings and those of the guests who landed on our Datai doorstep.

My dalliance at Datai wrapped up in 96, as the grand old lady was calling me back with her siren song....

Low hanging fruit

# Black Truffle Gnocchi, Aged Parmesan

Yield: 6 servings
Gnocchi:
9 ounces or 250 g cooked potato
3 tablespoons or 21 g all-purpose flour
3 egg yolks
1/2 black truffle, finely grated
Salt and ground black pepper, to taste
Garnish:
Veal jus
Shaved aged Parmesan cheese
Sliced black truffles
Chopped chives
Coarse salt
Extra-virgin olive oil
Method:
Place cooked potato through a ricer. Combine potato,
flour, egg yolks, truffle,
salt and pepper. Turn out onto a work surface, and knead
until smooth and blended.
Roll 1 tablespoon/5 g dough into ball; press with tines
of fork to flatten slightly.
Repeat with remaining dough.
In large saucepot, bring salted water to a boil.
Drop gnocchi into water, and cook until they float,
about 2 minutes.
Presentation:
Spoon 5 gnocchi into serving bowl. Top with veal jus.
Garnish with shaved Parmesan cheese, black truffles,
chives and coarse salt.
Drizzle with olive oil.

To John Burton Race, England
"You blazed the kitchen and kicked so much ass
that this is all I remember about you."

8

micro greens

To Mr. Philippe Padovani, Ritz Carlton,
Big Island of Hawaii
"I miss Hawaiian Vintage Chocolate."

breakfast crumble

8

Chef Norbert Chabot at the Château Laurier,
Parliament Hill, Ottawa.
"Mr. Chabot turning potatoes with you was a
pleasure and a pastime."

Chef Conny Andersson

To Wolfgang Von Wieser at the Four Seasons,
Toronto
'It was a pleasure helping you with Art Culinare
No. 4, hope you are enjoying the islands.'

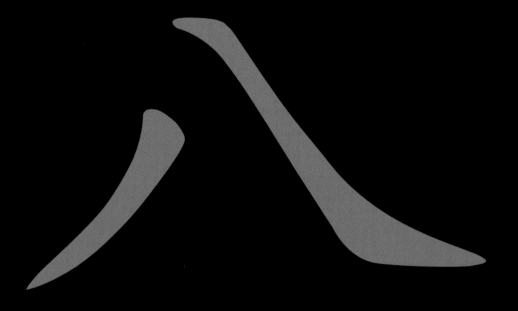

blackjack grilled rib-eye

# Maine Lobster Scotch Eggs

Yield: 2 servings
Scotch Eggs:
4 ounces or 112 g sea scallops
1 cup or 200 g cooked lobster, finely chopped
2 egg yolks
1 tablespoon or 3 g chopped chives
Salt and ground white pepper
8 hard-cooked quail eggs, peeled
1/2 cup or 60 g dried bread crumbs
Vegetable oil, for frying
Viking non-stick fry pans are perfect for delicate
foods with little or no oil. The food slides easily
out on to serving dish.
Dill Crème Fraiche:
1/2 cup or 125 ml crème fraiche 1 tablespoon or 3 g
chopped dill
Method:
Garnish:
Dill
Lemon Oil
Method:
Purée scallops in food processor or blender until
smooth. In large bowl, combine scallops,
lobster, egg yolks, chives, salt and pepper. Using
your fingers, shape some of the mixture around
a quail egg. Roll in bread crumbs,and repeat with remaining eggs.


Prepare Dill Crème Fraiche: Combine crème fraiche and
chopped dill until well blended.
In fryer or deep saucepan, heat oil to 375 F/190 C.
Fry scotch eggs 1 to 2 minutes or until golden. With
slotted spoon, remove onto paper towels to drain.
Presentation:
Arrange 4 scotch eggs on each serving plate.
Spoon some dill crème fraiche on plate; garnish with
dill. Drizzle with lemon oil.

# SINGAPORE ⊛9 6 ⊛
# RAFFLES
# ( THE RETURN )

There's an old saying 'You can't step twice into the
same river' and that certainly rang true upon my return
to Raffles. It was great to be home but there were some
challenges ahead namely, stepping into the bespoke
leather, steel-capped shoes of my mentor and
predecessor… The notorious Mr Knipp. It was a tough
gig.  Every day from dawn 'till midnight, no days off
and no rest for the wicked - But how could we rest,
with 14 restaurants to be maintained at the highest
standard and yes, some standards demanding
resurrection? Eventually I realized that life isn't
a Cinderella story, taking over a role isn't about
wearing someone else's shoes, it's about walking tall
to the Ball, in your own kick-ass pair.

To Mr Peter Knipp
"Your organizational skills are parallel to a German
clock, thank you for the insight. I know you always
like my Béarnaise but I will never give up the recipe."

In my Brave New World of Raffles, Mr MPS Puri and
Jennie Chua ran the Ministry of Everything. Jennie was
the Margaret Thatcher of the hotel.  They were a duo to
be reckoned with, inspiring our team to reach for and
win the Gold Medal from Food Hotel Asia. As the team
Captain, it was an achievement I will be eternally
proud of.  Leaving Raffles for a 2nd time was a
difficult decision to make, I was ready to take on a
new challenge a million miles from the rarified
atmosphere of Raffles, Singapore…

To Chef Joel Robuchon, Meilleur Ouvrier de France
"I am almost speechless when I think of Chef Joel and
the feeling of achievement after the dinner at the
Raffles Hotel for 250 guests that came together
without a hitch. I wish I would worked in the
restaurant Jamin with you, this is a memory I miss not
knowing."

# Baby Octopus Poke

Yield: 1 serving
3 to 4 whole baby octopus
1 tablespoon or 15 ml Johnny Walker Black Scotch
1 teaspoon or 5 ml red wine vinegar
1 teaspoon or 5 ml rice wine vinegar
1/2 teaspoon or 2.5 ml grated ginger
Pinch granulated sugar
1 tablespoon or 15 ml sesame oil 3
1 teaspoon or 2 g chopped dried seaweed 0 Chopped
chives, for garnish
Dried seaweed, for garnish
Method:
Place octopus in small saucepan, and add water to cover
Over high heat, bring to a boil. Reduce heat to low;
cover and simmer about 5 mintues. Drain well.
In medium bowl, combine Scotch, vinegars, ginger and
sugar. Whisk in sesame oil until blended. Add baby
octopus and seaweed; toss to mix well. Cover, and
refrigerate to marinate overnight.
Presentation:
Place marinated octopus in a serving bowl. Garnish with
chives and dried seaweed.

To Marc Veyrat, France
"Your signature black hat is what I remember
as well as the speed you worked with as you
sprinted around the kitchen with seamless
execution."

Shellfish platter

# Maine Lobster Truffle Burger

Yield: 2 servings

Burger:
8 ounces or 227 g cooked lobster meat, chopped
2 ounces or 57 g cooked foie gras
1/4 cup or 50 ml heavy cream
1 tablespoon or 15 ml red onion marmalade
1 tablespoon or 5 g chopped chives
Salt and ground black pepper
1 tablespoon or 15 ml olive oil

Method:
Garnish:
Veal jus
Black truffle slices
1/2 cup or 20 g micro celery leaves Shaved Parmesan cheese
Extra-virgin olive oil Coarse salt
In medium bowl, combine lobster, foie gras, heavy cream, red
onion marmalade, chives, salt and pepper until well mixed. Shape
mixture into two "burgers", about 1 inch/2.5 cm thick.
In 12-inch/30.5 cm skillet over medium heat, warm oil. Add the
burgers, and cook 5 to 8 minutes or until cooked through,
turning once.
Presentation:
Place lobster burger in shallow bowl; top with veal jus. Top
with truffle slices, micro celery leaves and shaved Parmesan
cheese. Drizzle with olive oil, and sprinkle with coarse salt.

# "Jean-Louis Style" Foie Gras

Yield: 8 servings
1 lobe of foie gras, about 1 pound or 450 grams, cleaned
Salt and ground black pepper
5 shallots, thinly sliced
Herbs, for garnish
Kumquat Marmalade, optional
Method: 5 Preheat oven to 375 F/190 C. Season foie gras
with salt and pepper. 8
Over high heat, heat large, oven-proof skillet.
Add foie gras; brown well on each side.
Add shallots to skillet. Place skillet in oven.
Roast 10 minutes.
Drain off fat, reserving for another use.
Continue cooking 5 minutes longer or until tender.
Remove foie gras from oven.
Presentation:
Place foie gras on serving platter. Let rest 5 to 10
minutes before serving. Garnish with herbs. If desired,
serve with Kumquat Marmalade.

Chef Louis Tay, Singapore

# Pan-Seared Fillet of Red Mullet, Yellow Frisee, Lemon Oil

Yield: 2 servings
Red Mullet:
2 tablespoons or 30 ml olive oil
3 pieces or 300 g red mullet or 2 pieces or 280 g red
snapper fillets
Salt and ground white pepper
Frisee Salad:
4 ounces or 113 g frisee
2 ounces or 57 g microgreens
Lemon oil
Baby Heirloom Salad:
8 ounces or 227 g heirloom cherry tomatoes, halved
Chopped chives
Garnish:
Lemon oil
Chervil Leaves
1/2 cup or 50 g pitted black olives, halved
Method:
Prepare Red Mullet: In 12-inch/30.5 cm skillet over
medium-high heat, warm oil.
Add fish fillets, and cook until lightly browned on both
sides.
Season with salt and pepper.
Prepare Frisee Salad: Toss frisee, microgreens, and
lemon oil to mix well.
Prepare Baby Heirloom Salad: Toss tomatoes and chives to
mix well.
Presentation:
Place red mullet fillets on plate. Drizzle with lemon
oil; garnish with chervil.
Arrange Frisee Salad, Baby Heirloom Salad and olives on
plate.

# Braised Lamb Shank, Sweetbreads,Swiss Chard, Tomato Jus

Yield: 6 servings

Lamb Shanks:
6 lamb shanks, about 6 pounds or 2.8 kg
Salt and ground black pepper
2 tablespoons or 30 ml vegetable oil
2 tomatoes, chopped
1 carrot, chopped
1 onion, chopped
1 large garlic clove, minced
2 sprigs thyme
2 cups dry red wine
1 cup or 250 ml veal stock
10 ounces or 284 g caul fat

Swiss Chard:
2 tablespoons or 30 ml olive oil
1 bunch Swiss chard, cut into 2-inch or 5 cm pieces
1 garlic clove, minced

Farce:
1 carrot, finely chopped
1 stalk celery, finely chopped
1 leek, finely chopped
10 ounces or 284 g chicken mousse
8 ounces or 227 g veal sweetbreads,
cleaned, blanched and chopped
2 ounces or 57 g black truffles, finely chopped
2 teaspoons or 2 g oregano leaves
Salt and ground black pepper

Garnish:
1 large tomato, finely chopped,Herb butter.Thyme sprigs

Method:
Preheat oven to 300ºF/150ºC. Season lamb shanks with salt and pepper. In large, deep skillet over high heat,
warm oil. Add lamb shanks; cook until well browned on all sides. Remove into roasting pan.
In skillet with remaining drippings over medium heat, cook tomatoes, carrot, onion, garlic and thyme
5 to 10 minutes. Add wine and veal stock. Cover, and braise 90 minutes or until lamb is just tender.
Remove from oven. Cool until easy to handle. Or, refrigerate overnight until ready to use.
Prepare farce: In boiling water, blanch separately carrot, celery and leek, and cool. In large bowl, combine
chicken mousse, sweetbreads, truffles, blanched vegetables, oregano, salt and pepper to mix well.
Thinly slice lamb meat from shanks. Line six 4-inch/10 cm metal rings with lamb. Spoon or pipe farce into
center of each round. Cover and refrigerate rings 1 hour or until slightly set.
Preheat oven to 350ºF/177ºC. Carefully remove metal rings from lamb. Wrap each piece with caul fat.
In 12-inch/30.5 cm skillet over medium-high heat, cook lamb until well browned on all sides.
Place in oven, and roast 20 minutes.
Prepare Swiss Chard: In large saucepan over medium-high heat, warm oil. Add Swiss chard and garlic, and cook until Swiss chardis tender, stirring occasionally.

Presentation:
Place Swiss chard lamb in serving dish; add lamb shank.
Garnish with tomato, herb butter and thyme sprigs.

# Duck Leg Confit, Potato-Apple Gratin, Brussels Sprouts

Salad Chopped tomatoes 3 Prepare Duck Confit: In glass
baking dish, combine salt, sugar, pepper, garlic, thyme and
orange peel.
Add duck legs; rub with mixture. Cover and refrigerate at
least 12 hours.
Remove duck legs from mixture, and rinse well in cold water.
Dry duck legs. Cover duck legs with vegetable oil or duck
fat; refrigerate until ready to cook.
Preheat oven to 200°F/105°. Bake duck legs 3 hours or until
tender.
Prepare Potato-Apple Gratin: Preheat oven to 350°F/180°.
Layer potatoes, apples, cheese and garlic in large, greased
baking dish. Add heavy cream and salt and pepper to taste.
Bake 40 minutes or until potatoes are tender and lightly
golden. Remove from oven. Carefully weigh down potato mix-
ture with another greased baking dish to fit. Cover, and re-
frigerate until ready to serve.
Prepare Brussels Sprout Salad: Remove outer green leaves
from Brussels sprouts to make 2 cups. Blanch for 30 seconds.
Drain and cool. Toss with walnut vinaigrette.
Sprinkle with walnuts and chives.
Presentation:
Heat duck legs and potato-apple gratin.
Plate a duck leg on serving plate.
Drizzle with armagnac jus and chopped tomatoes. Serve with
Potato-Apple Gratin and Brussels Sprout Salad.
Duck Leg Confit, Potato-Apple Gratin, Brussels Sprout Salad
Yield: 4 servings

Potato-Apple Gratin:
4 Yukon Gold potatoes, peeled and thinly sliced
2 Granny Smith apples, peeled, cored and thinly sliced 1 cup
or 115 g shredded Gruyere cheese
1 garlic clove, minced
2 cups or 500 ml heavy cream Salt and ground black pepper
Brussels Sprout Salad:
8 ounces or 170 g Brussels sprouts Walnut Vinaigrette
2 tablespoons or 20 g chopped walnuts 1 tablespoon or 3 g
chopped chives
Garnish:
Chicken jus seasoned with Armagnac 1
Duck Confit:
1 cup or 100 g rock salt
1/2 cup or 50 g granulated sugar
2 teaspoons or 8 g cracked black pepper
2 garlic cloves, crushed
1 teaspoon or 2 g thyme leaves
1 tablespoon or 9 g grated orange peel
4 duck legs
3 tablespoons or 45 ml vegetable oil or melted duck fat

# Beef Tenderloin, Potato Skins, Soy Butter

Yield: 4 servings
Potato Skins:
2 large Idaho potatoes, washed Vegetable oil
Coarse salt
Beef Tenderloin:
4 (6-ounce or 170 g) fillet mignons, each about 2 inches
or 5 cm thick
Salt and ground black pepper
Soy Butter:
1/4 cup or 50 ml soy sauce
3 tablespoons or 45 ml red wine vinegar

2 tablespoons or 30 ml chicken stock
3 garlic cloves, chopped

juice of 1/2 lemon
4 ounces or 113 g butter
1 tablespoon or 3 g chopped chives Salt and ground white
pepper
Vegetables:
1 pound or 450 g mixed green and wax beans
2 large carrots, peeled and cut into 1-inch or 2.5 cm
diagonal slices 1 Salt and ground black pepper 4
Chopped chives, for garnish

Method:
Prepare Soy Butter:
In small saucepan over high heat, simmer soy sauce, red
wine vinegar, stock, garlic and lemon until mixture is
reduced by half. Gradually whisk in butter.
Add chives, salt and pepper. Keep warm.

Prepare Potato Skins: Cut /4-inch/6.5 mm slices from
each side of the potatoes.
Discard insides of potatoes. Blanch potato slices in
boiling water 1 to 2 minutes. Pat dry with paper towels.
In fryer or deep saucepan, heat oil to 375°F/190°C.
Fry potatoes about 3 minutes or until golden brown.
With slotted spoon, remove to paper towels to drain.
Sprinkle with coarse salt. Keep warm.
Prepare beef tenderloins: Preheat grill to high.
Season tenderloins with salt and pepper. Grill beef
until desired doneness.
Blanch vegetables in boiling salted water until
tender. Season with salt and pepper.
Presentation:
Arrange vegetables on serving plate. Slice each fillet;
arrange on vegetables. Top with potato skins. Drizzle
with soy butter. Garnish with chives.

# Herb-Crusted Rack of Lamb, Fork-Crushed Sweet Potatoes, Mushroom Jus

Yield: 2 servings
Lamb:
6-rib rack of lamb
Salt and cracked black pepper
1 tablespoon or 15 ml vegetable oil
2 slices day-old bread, crusts removed
1 tablespoon or 5 g chopped parsley
2 tablespoons or 30 ml coarse-grain mustard
Sautéed Mushrooms:
1 tablespoon or 15 ml olive oil
8 ounces or 225 g assorted mushrooms, such as chanterelle or oyster
2 shallots, finely chopped
2 scallions, cut into 3-inch or 7.5 cm pieces
Accompaniments:
Fork-Crushed Sweet Potatoes
Mushroom jus, for garnish
Method:
Prepare Lamb: Preheat oven to 350ºF/180ºC. Season lamb with salt and pepper.
In 12-inch/30.5 cm skillet over medium-high heat, warm oil.
Add rack of lamb; brown well on all sides. Remove from skillet.
In food processor, blend bread slices and parsley until well blended.
Spread mustard on fat-side of lamb to cover; pat crumb mixture into mustard.
Bake 10 to 12 minutes or until lamb is desired doneness.
Prepare Mushrooms: In 12-inch/30.5 cm skillet over medium heat, warm oil.
Add mushrooms, shallots and scallions, and cook until tender, stirring occasionally.
Presentation:
Place 3 lamb ribs on plate. Serve with mushrooms, sweet potatoes and mushroom jus.

**8**

To George Blanc
"You helping me understand Bresse chicken and
how to cook this dish is timeless".

Ginger Pistachio Moustache

To Stan West, Niagara Falls, Canada.
"Thank you for the experience, I know I was high
maintenance but we took care of business."

Tucker Box

8

"I met Grant in Singapore back in 1994 when I joined
Raffles Hotel as the Maitre d' at the Raffles Grill.
We worked very hard with great synergy, yet had plenty
of laughs and tremendous fun. It was indeed a pleasure
working together with Grant and probably some of the
best times I've had! To this day, every time we meet,
we still share our fond memories of our good ol' days.
We have remained good friends ever since."

HANSJOERG MEIER
General Manager
The Setai, South Beach Miami

"During my 29 years in the high end clothing industry, I have come across the who is who, amassing thousands, and I found they have one thing in common. Gravitating to whomever professes passion in what they do and Grant MacPherson wrote the book about passion for the culinary industry during his tenure "

MICHAEL RESLAN, Clothing Atelier, NYC

Las Vegas farmers market

To Werner Watzdorf of the Four Seasons,
Vancouver
"Mr. Werner, what's our next concert and do
you want a pepper steak?"

8

Golden beets

100

# Curried Cashews

Yield: 1 pound or 450 g
1 pound or 450 g raw cashews
3 tablespoons or 20 g Madras curry powder
1 1/2 teaspoons or 3 g ground cumin
1 1/2 teaspoons or 3 g ground anise
1 teaspoon or 3 g chili powder
2 tablespoons or 30 ml water
1 1/2 teaspoons or 3 g cornstarch
Peanut oil, for frying
Sea salt
Method:
In large bowl, combine cashews, curry powder, cumin,
anise and chili powder; toss to coat well.
In small bowl, combine water and cornstarch; toss with
cashews to coat. Let stand 2 hours.
In fryer or deep saucepan, heat oil to 375° F/190° C.
Fry cashews 4 to 5 minutes, or until golden brown.
With slotted spoon, remove onto paper towels to drain.
Immediately sprinkle cashews with salt to taste.
Cool completely.
Store in tightly covered container or airtight plastic
bag up to 2 weeks.

# Grey Goose - Pacific Salmon, Mustard Dressing

Yield: 2 servings
Salmon:
1 fillet wild salmon or pink trout, 6 to 8 ounces or 170
to 225 g 2 tablespoons or 30 ml Grey Goose Vodka
1 tablespoon or 15 ml coarse-grain Dijon mustard
1 tablespoon or 3 g chopped dill
4 to 5 black peppercorns, cracked
1/4 teaspoon or 2 g coarse salt
Dill sprigs, for garnish
Mustard Dressing:
2 tablespoons or 30 ml coarse-grain Dijon mustard
2 tablespoons or 30 ml crème fraiche
1 tablespoon or 3 g chopped dill
1 teaspoon or 5 ml lime juice
Salt and ground black pepper, to taste
Method:
Prepare Salmon: Place salmon in glass baking dish or
bowl; 5 sprinkle with vodka. Let stand 30 minutes.
Meanwhile, preheat oven to 275 F/140 C.
In small bowl, combine mustard, dill, peppercorns and
salt.
Remove salmon from baking dish and place on untreated
cedar plank. Place plank on baking sheet. Spread top of
salmon with mustard mixture. Bake 6 to 8 minutes or
until fish flakes easily when tested with a fork.
Prepare Mustard Dressing: Combine mustard, crème
fraiche, dill, lime juice, salt and pepper until well
mixed.
Presentation:
Serve salmon with Mustard Dressing. Garnish with dill.

White Truffle auction Lanesborough Hotel

Las Vegas farmers market

"Having known Grant MacPherson for the last 15 years,
I wholeheartedly and with confidence recognize his
full knowledge and capabilities in everything
essential to the food industry and all aspects of the
culinary profession".
DE RUYTER O. BUTLER, A.I.A, Executive VP
of Architecture, Wynn Design and Development

Red mullet Scottish corn beef hash

# VEGAS 098 -BELLAGIO

When Siro Maccioni, Gamal Aziz and Elizabeth Blau put
in the call, you answer - And that's how I found myself
at the iconic Bellagio, swapping one jungle for
another… Neon decadence trumps Tropical splendor.
Hello Vegas! I have just entered Sin city. Inebriated
individuals zig-zagging the street all hours of the
day, the scantily clad ladies and the constant offering
of 'adult services' was just all part of the scenery.

Sweltering in the relentless desert heat, my first
thought was "Sweet Jesus - What the fuck have I done?!"
On 4th July 1998 I stood in line with Jay James, Master
Sommelier for two hours waiting to be served at a
buffet filled with plastic death-shrouded fruit bowls
and vegetables as limp as the apathetic service
standards. My second thought was "OK there are
problems, so it's time to find solutions."

To Wolfgang Puck
"Meeting you when we cooked your fiftieth birthday in
1999 at Bellagio was phenomenal. The team that you have
put together in Las Vegas under David Robbins direction
is unrivalled."

# Beverly Hills Cheese

Yield: 2 to 4 servings
Wedge of Tomme de Savoie
Wedge of English Stilton
Wedge of Crottin de Chavignol
Wedge of Aged Gouda
Wedge of Fromage de Lambert
1 small bunch Champagne grapes
Lady apples
Melba Toast

# Tandoori of Pork Tenderloin,

Egg-Fried Rice, Pomegranate Jus
Yield: 4 servings
Tandoori Pork :
1 pound or 450 g pork tenderloin
1 cup or 250 ml yogurt
1 tablespoon or 15 ml lime juice
1 tablespoon or 9 g tandoori spice rub (or mix chili
powder and ground cumin)
Egg-Fried Rice:
3 cups or 170 g cold, cooked rice
4 large eggs
1/2 teaspoon or 3 g salt
3 tablespoons or 45 ml vegetable oil, divided
1 cup or 100 g green peas
1 tablespoon or 15 ml soy sauce
1 tablespoon or 4 g chopped scallions
Pomegranate Jus:
1/2 cup or 125 ml chicken stock
1 tablespoon or 15 ml red wine vinegar
1 tablespoon or 15 ml Dijon mustard
2 tablespoons or 10 g pomegranate seeds
Garnish:
Salt and ground black pepper
Chopped mint
Method:
Prepare tandoori pork: In medium bowl, combine yogurt,
lime juice and tandoori spice rub;
add pork and turn to coat. Cover, and refrigerate
overnight.
Preheat oven to 350°F/180°C. Remove pork from marinade.
In 12-inch/30.5 cm skillet over medium-high heat,
cook pork tenderloin until well browned on all sides,
turning occasionally. Place pork in oven.
Cook 15 minutes or until internal temperature reaches
160°F/71°C.
Prepare Egg-Fried Rice: Whisk eggs and salt together.
In 12-inch/30.5 cm skillet over medium heat,
warm 1 tablespoon/15 ml oil. Add eggs, and cook until
set, scrambling in pan.
Add remaining 2 tablespoons/30 ml oil to skillet.
Add rice; cook until grains are coated with oil,
about 3 minutes. Stir in peas, soy sauce and scallions;
heat through. Stir in eggs.
Prepare Pomegranate Jus: In small bowl, combine chicken
stock, red wine vinegar and mustard until well blended;
stir in pomegranate seeds.
Presentation:
Slice pork tenderloin; arrange on platter.
Drizzle with pomegranate jus.
Serve with fried rice. Season with salt and pepper.
Garnish with chopped mint.

"Grant is a culinary artist; a purist of the highest
order...
He turns the elegance of simplicity into an art form
for discerning palates while blending the freshest
ingredients. Unflappable, pleasant under pressure and
solution oriented ... a delight who quickly grasps the
'big picture' and performs impeccably."
PAT KERR, America's celebrated Fashion and
Bridal Designer

Baby grilled octopus, saffron rouille

118

Niagara Beet salad

Maine Lobster, endangered species

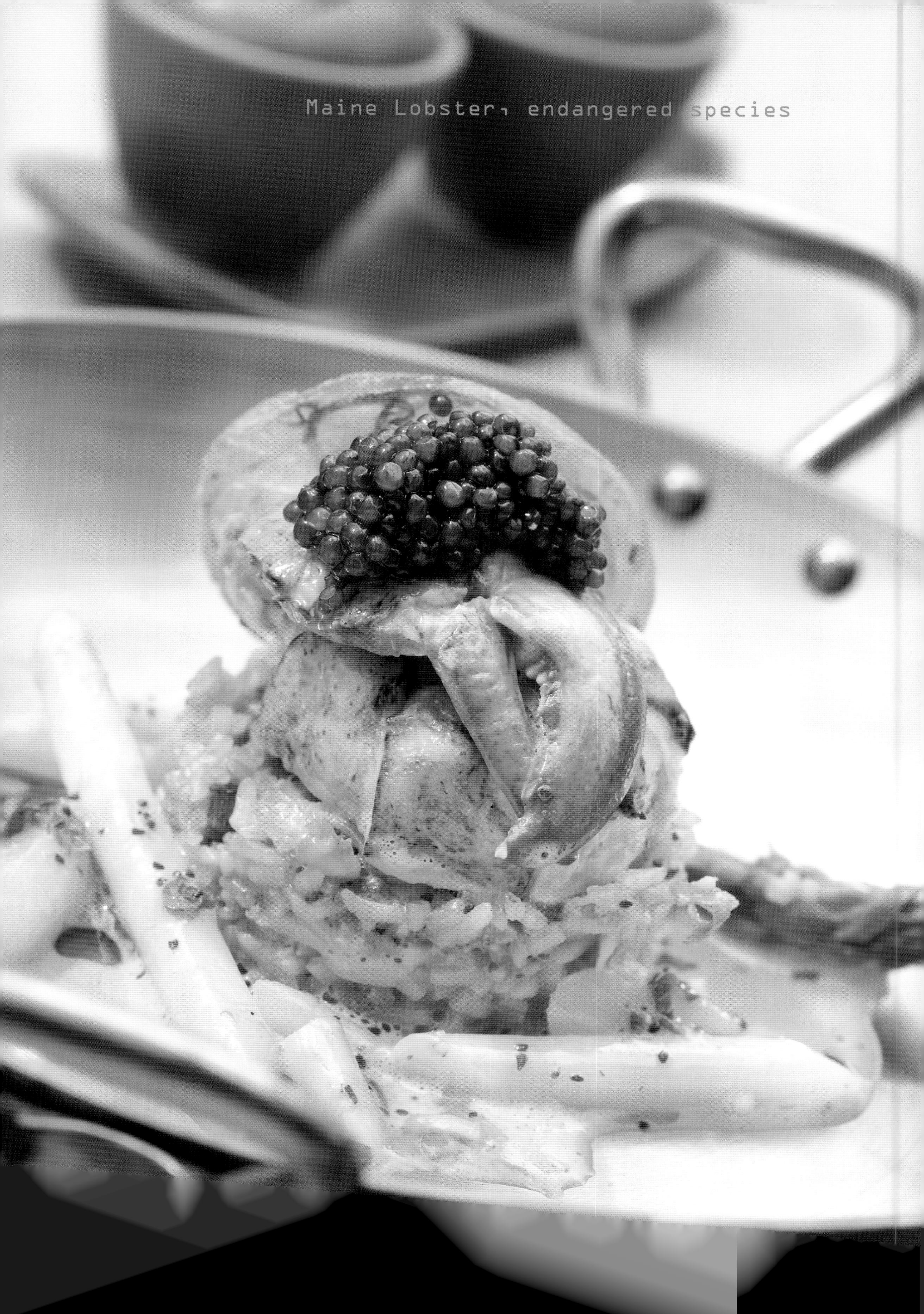

# Flight of Seasonal Breakfast Juices

Yield: 6 servings
4 cups or 600 g seedless watermelon chunks
1 golden ripe pineapple, peeled, cored, cut into chunks
4 large carrots, peeled
4 juice oranges, halved
2 pink or ruby grapefruits, halved
Method:
With immersion blender or in a blender, blend pineapple
until smooth.
Refrigerate juice until ready to serve.
With immersion blender or in a blender, blend watermelon
chunks until
smooth. Refrigerate juice until ready to serve.
Using a juicer, juice carrots. Refrigerate juice until
ready to serve.
Juice grapefruits. Refrigerate juice until ready to
serve.
Juice oranges. Refrigerate until ready to serve.
Presentation:
Serve juices in chilled glasses.

Bill Milne, Grant and Fred Carl Jr.

"Grant MacPherson is one of the most talented chefs
I've ever known. He approaches food with a gentle
intensity that translates into amazing results. The
dishes he creates are a celebration of his lifetime of
culinary exploration around the world, giving him a
truly global, firsthand perspective on cuisines of many
cultures. Grant MacPherson has quietly become one of
the most respected and highly regarded chefs in the
world."

FRED CARL JR.

James Beard acknowledgement 2000

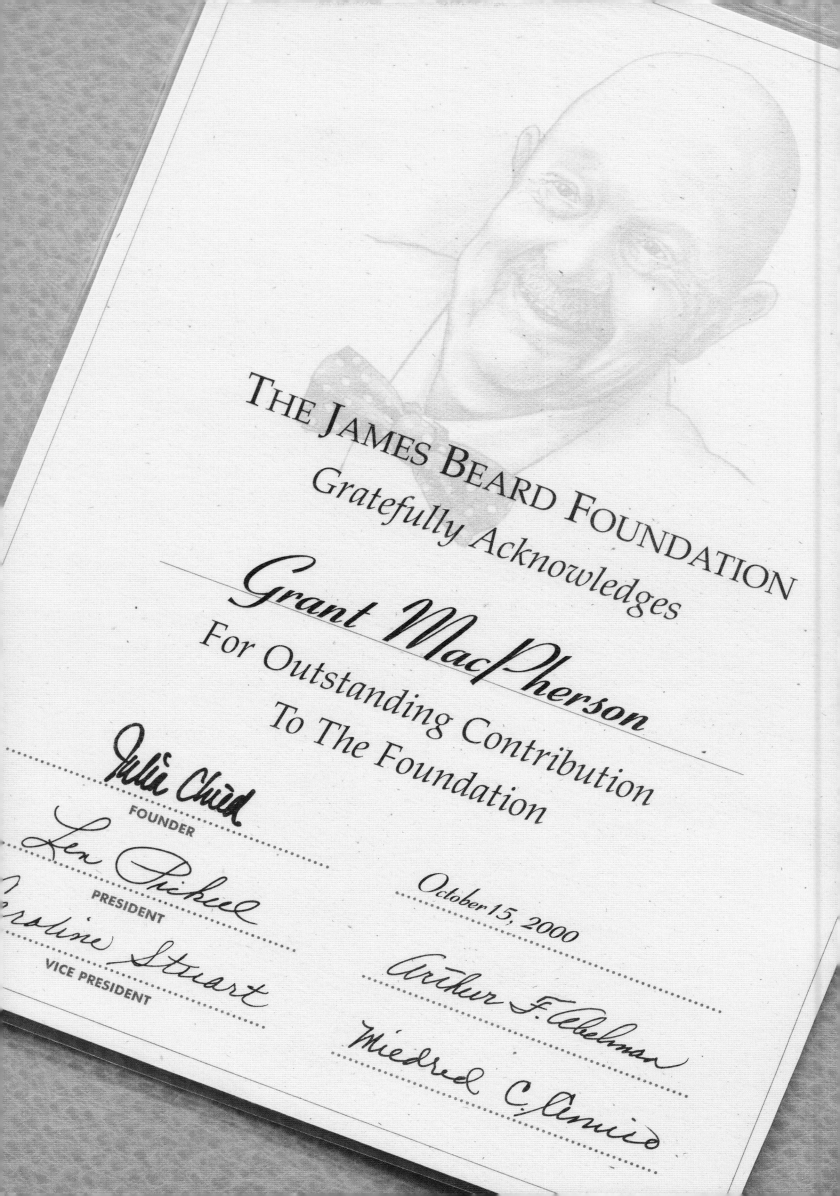

# THE JAMES BEARD FOUNDATION
## Gratefully Acknowledges

### Grant MacPherson

For Outstanding Contribution
To The Foundation

*Julia Child*
FOUNDER

*Len Pickel*
PRESIDENT

*Caroline Stuart*
VICE PRESIDENT

October 15, 2000

*Arthur F. Abelman*

*Miedred C. Amico*

Jean-Phillipe Maury, Meilleur Ouvrier de France, Master Patissiere and Chocolatiere entered the scene and we were like a chicken and a duck trying to communicate. Language barrier, opposite personalities and conflicting egos - But hell, did we take care of business! For all its glitz, Vegas was crying out for a little glamour and J.P. knocked their socks off. Differences aside, our number one rule was No Politics and as our team grew strong, so did our reputation. The kitchen was about volume, obscene and unrelenting volume. Feeding the masses and occasionally the celebs like Slash, Billy Gibbons, Dennis Rodman and my personal favorite, meeting the glorious Julia Roberts during the filming of Oceans Eleven. Throughout all this mayhem, celebrity rock star chef, Kerry Simon AKA the great white buffalo became a good friend.

Bellagio was a little bumpy on the way out. as I wandered down to the Desert Inn.

To Chef Jean-Philippe Maury,
Meilleur Ouvrier de France
"Jean-Phillipe your pastries and visual presentation was spectacular and you will agree we spent a lot of time yelling at each other but at the end of the day, Were we ever late for a function?".

Chef Ewart Wardhaugh

# Snake-River Kobe Ribs

Garlic Oil
Yield: 6 servings
8 pounds or 3.6 kg beef short ribs, cleaned
6 cups or 1.4 liters chicken stock
2 large carrots, coarsely chopped
2 celery stalks, coarsely chopped
1 large onion, coarsely chopped
2 large garlic cloves, peeled
Salt and ground black pepper
2 tablespoons or 30 ml olive oil
2 garlic cloves, sliced
Thyme sprigs, for garnish
Coarse salt, for garnish
Method:
In large pan over high heat, bring beef short ribs,
chicken stock,
carrots, celery, onion and garlic to a boil. Reduce heat
to low;
simmer 25 minutes or until ribs are just tender.
Drain well, discarding vegetables and liquid.
Preheat grill to high. With paring knife, score fat-side
of each rib in a diagonal pattern. Season ribs with salt
and pepper.
Grill ribs 10 to 12 minutes, turning frequently.
In small saucepan over medium heat, warm oil.
Add garlic, and cook until lightly browned,
stirring frequently. Remove garlic.
Presentation:
Arrange ribs on platter;
drizzle with garlic oil.
Garnish with thyme sprigs and coarse salt.

Bellagio fountains

# MACAU 003 -WYNN

Wynn Macau... The far eastern apparition from the mind
of Steve Wynn, megastar magnate. I should just stop
there. But I won't.

Exciting times, this was unexplored territory being
built on recycled landfill. Up to my neck in creative
chaos I met DeRuyter Butler and Todd Nisbet, the
visionary architect and builder respectively, behind
this heavenly creature. As one of the world's leading
luxury hotels emerged from the rubble and disorder, so
too did long-lasting friendships.  Mr Peter Find
stepped up to the helm and ran an extreme team of raw
talent and fresh open minds ready for a rock n roll
kung fu hospitality adventure.

Opening night on September 5, 2006 we organized and
executed Dinner for 688 guests. Menu included Belon
Oysters, Golden Ocietra Caviar, U.S.D.A Prime Beef and
the sexiest chocolates I've ever seen. Over 20,000
people lined up for the chance to check out the
sumptuous fit-out, let alone a seat and much less a
bed!  Like a mad cross between orchestral conductor and
rock concert manager, Ian Michael Coughlan arrived
later as President and started running the show.

To the late Mr. Jean-Louis Palladin, Watergate Hotel,
Washington D.C.
"You sir, helped me relocate to Las Vegas and changed
my life and if I could, I would play one more game of
pool with you."

Wynn Las Vegas walk-in freezer -2005

Malaysian Chicken satays

8

"I've had a tremendous amount of respect and admiration for Grant MacPherson since we first cooked together at a fundraiser with our good friend Jean-Louis Palladin. Since then his success at running food and beverage programs at some of the best hotels nationally and internationally has been unparalleled and the care and commitment he puts into good food and his cuisine has been recognized the world over. We are on the same wavelength and I count him among my closest friends and peers".

Chef JOHO, Everest, Brasserie JO, Eiffel Tower Restaurant, Paris Club

Ratatouille

# LAS VEGAS 006 -WYNN

During all the exquisite Macau mayhem Steve invited me
to his Vegas namesake. If Las Vegas was a porn shop
cabinet filled with bling, and scratchy flash - Steve
Wynn is the canary diamond. Once again I found myself
working alongside the sophisticated Lady Blau, flying
around the world on a treasure hunt recruitment drive
for the best, newly minted culinary talent and concepts
money and reputation could buy. Money talks - Wealth
whispers. The opening environment for Wynn Las Vegas
was simply astonishing in its excess and in its
excessive consumption. We fed over 30,000 people in the
first 24 hours. Meeting the quiet approval for opening
night fare enjoyed by the likes of Mr Donald Trump and
Richard Branson was a milestone... Appreciation from
palates no doubt bombarded with excellence, every
morsel of every day is something to be proud of. It was
at the right time and I might have even over-stayed my
10 years with the Wynn family organization but they'll
be under my skin for the rest of my life.


To Chef Bernard Ibarra, Four Seasons, Toronto.
"We both enjoying great careers in Las Vegas."

Okada

Butter chicken

"It was my pleasure to bring Grant to the USA and have
the opportunity to work together opening the Bellagio.
His work ethic and ideas were of world standard and
class and helped to define the entire food and beverage
program. Dining in Las Vegas was going through a major
change which meant we were part of an evolutionary
experience. The move to Wynn was yet another enormous
and a hugely challenging project yet it felt seamless
when travelling and working with Grant. The policy on
the team was all about hard work and integrity."

ELIZABETH BLAU,

CEO of Blau + Associates

The Buffet

# Pecan-Nut Cheesecake, Blueberry Compote

Yield: 6 servings
Cheesecake:
Butter, for pan
8 ounces or 227 g cream cheese, softened
2 large eggs
3/4 cup or 150 g granulated sugar
1 teaspoon or 5 ml vanilla extract
Blueberry Compote:
1 cup or 140 g blueberries
1/4 cup or 50 g granulated sugar
1/4 cup or 50 ml Fiji water
1/4 cup or 50 ml balsamic vinegar
1 cinnamon stick
1 star anise
1 teaspoon or 2 g grated orange peel
Pinch salt
Garnish:
1/4 cup or 42 g finely chopped pecans, toasted
1 dragon fruit, peeled and sliced
Whole pecans
Method:
Prepare Cheesecake: Preheat oven to 350°F/180°C. Line
9- by 9-inch/ 22 cm by 22 cm baking pan with foil;
butter foil. In mixer at high speed, beat cream cheese,
eggs, sugar and vanilla until light and fluffy.
Pour mixture into prepared pan.
Bake in a water bath, about 40 minutes or until cheesecake is set. Remove to rack; cool completely.
Refrigerate until ready to use.
Prepare Blueberry Compote: In medium saucepan, combine
blueberries, sugar, water, vinegar, cinnamon,
anise, orange peel and salt. Over high heat, bring to a
boil.
Reduce heat to low; simmer 5 minutes until sauce is
thickened, stirring frequently.
Presentation:
Lift foil to remove cheesecake from pan. With buttered
3-inch round cutter, cut cheesecake into 6 rounds.
Roll outside edges of cheesecake in chopped pecans.
Place each cheesecake on a serving plate.
Serve with blueberry compote.
Garnish with dragon fruit and whole pecans.

# BARBADOS 008 - SANDY LANE

Irish billionaire Dermot Desmond loved Sandy Lane like
I love cooking.  In '97 he fought a classic battle for
integrity, halting a multinational in their tracks who
were determined to destroy its iconic façade.  In '98
he closed the doors for a comprehensive and
compassionate rebuild, the luxury 1960's Colonial
plantation landmark re-opening on St Patrick's Day
2001.
I got the call in late '07 and the decision was easy,
starting on January 8 2008, who was I to resist a gig
in paradise?! The refined opulence and eccentric
British history of Sandy Lane was a welcome contrast to
the frenetic, manufactured thrill of Vegas. 1000 acres
of palm trees and 3 manicured golf courses, 108 keys of
turquoise splash and silver shimmer. Like I said,..
Paradise.

In the beginning, the place was a veritable energy
vacuum, enthusiasm and creativity was flat-lining...
After a few months of tweaking and adjusting the
levels, the fire began to burn a little hotter, more
intense. We discovered many gifted Bajan chefs and
built a team from scratch, teaching them to turn raw
talent into execution perfection. Sandy Lane was
humming again and for anywhere between 5,000 - 25,000
dollars a night, let's face it - Perfection was an
expectation, not an option.

Sandy Lane was a magnet for an eclectic menagerie of
truly Cool-Brittania guests including friend Simon
Cowell, a self-confessed Shepherd's Pie addict and
Sir Phillip Green, whose penchant was for char-grilled
prime steak and my signature ripped potatoes... I miss
Michael Winner and our tradition of afternoon waffle
indulgence.

To Rudy Mack of the Four Seasons, Toronto.
"Mr. Rudy your unforgettable duck consume is etched
into my minds fabric and I still use your theories
today and it tastes just like yesterday."

Big hook, Small fish

"I have always enjoyed creating restaurants with Grant.
He is very practical when it comes to operations and at
the cutting edge of culinary excellence with a great
attitude towards dining drama and aesthetics.
It's both creative and magical working with him as for
every restaurant we have created, has become a success.
Most of all...... we always have great fun....
an absolute ball of a time!!!!!"
ALBURN WILLIAM,

President,
Creative Kitchen Planners, Malaysia

Bajan Blue, Barbados

Red snapper

Tuna tartar

Local Chicken, ripped potato

Designer Todd-Avery Lenahan

# Roasted Baby Root Vegetables

Yield: 4 servings
1 pound or 450 g yellow and orange baby
carrots, peeled
1 pound or 450 g golden and red baby beets,
peeled
3 tablespoons or 45 ml olive oil
2 tablespoons or 10 g chopped parsley
Salt and ground black pepper
Method:
Preheat oven to 375°F/190°C.
Bring a pot of salted water to a boil,
blanch separately carrots and beets 5 to 10
minutes; drain.
In roasting pan or large oven-proof skillet,
toss vegetables with olive oil, parsley, salt
and pepper to taste.
Roast 10 to 15 minutes or until tender,
stirring occasionally.

# Balmain Bugs, Tarragon Butter

Yield: 2 servings
Heirloom Tomato Salad:
1 pint red and yellow heirloom tomatoes, each cut in half
1 tablespoon or 15 ml extra-virgin olive oil
1 shallot, thinly sliced
1/2 teaspoon or 4 ml red wine vinegar
Lobster:
2 slipper lobsters (Balmain Bugs), halved lengthwise and cleaned
1/4 cup or 50 ml extra-virgin olive oil
Sea salt
Tarragon sprigs
Tarragon Butter:
1/4 cup or 56 g butter
1 tablespoon or 3 g minced tarragon
Garnish:
Tarragon sprigs
Heirloom Tomato Salad (below)
Method:
Prepare Heirloom Tomato Salad: Toss tomatoes with olive oil, shallots and red wine vinegar.
Prepare Lobster: Preheat grill to medium-high.
Brush cut-side of lobsters with olive oil and salt.
Place shell-side down on rack on grill. Top lobster halves with tarragon sprigs.
Cover lobsters with large roasting pan.
Cook until flesh is opaque, about 10 minutes.
Prepare Tarragon Butter: In small saucepan over medium heat,
melt butter; stir in tarragon.
Presentation:
Arrange lobster halves and additional tarragon sprigs on platter. Drizzle with tarragon butter.
Serve with Heirloom Tomato Salad.

Mini burgers

To  Fred Carl Jr, Founder of
Viking Range Corporation
"Mr. Carl you are also the Chairman, President
and Chief Executive Officer of Viking Range
Corporation, you are so hands on with your
business which always won my admiration.
An industry leader in the manufacturing of
premium kitchen appliances for the home, I have
not only admired your success and quality
products but also find it an honour to be an
ambassador for Viking and a personal friend of
yours."

8

# LOS ANGELES 010 - RUSTICA

I promised myself I wouldn't leave anything out of the story so let's talk about Rustica. Exclusive, subversive, radical Rustica. With an address like Fashion Island, Newport Beach Ca. you'd be forgiven for assuming this might be just another Californian Wine Bistro. But you'd be wrong. And you'd be lost. Great location, beautifully designed, amazing talent, a hidden door, word of mouth and follow the line of salivating food groupies. My mission (should I choose to accept it) was to maintain the inertia. No problem. Let's leave all the politics at the door, but as the time passed they found their way inside.

To Chef Raymond Blanc
"I made a mistake by turning down the opportunity to work with you in Oxford, England and you are the only two star Michelin Chef in the world who still truly deserves three."

Fashion Island, an iconic outdoor shopping center that caters to the thriving resort market, coastal communities and affluent residents from throughout Southern California.

**8**

Menu number 1 Rustica, Fashion Island California

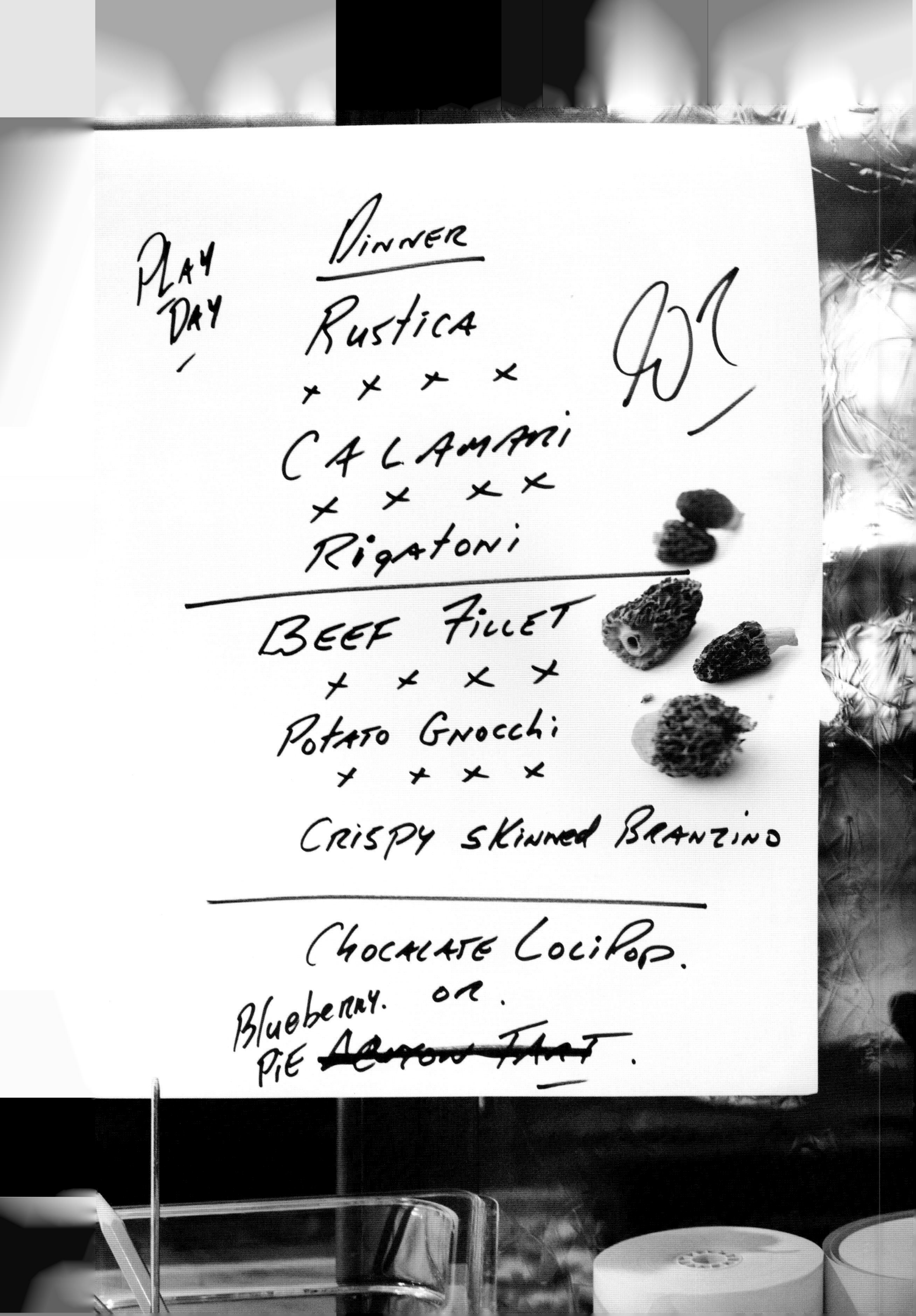

PLAY
DAY

Dinner

Rustica

+ + + +

CALAMARI

+ + + +

Rigatoni

BEEF FILLET

+ + + +

Potato Gnocchi

+ + + +

Crispy skinned Branzino

Chocolate Lolipop.

Blueberry.   or.

Pie ~~Lemon Tart~~.

# THE MERRYWELL

Crown, Melbourne.
Austrailia

A new beginning.

THE MERRYWELL

8

"One of the greatest skills of a chef is identifying the
finest ingredients and allowing that ingredient to speak
for itself. Grant is a man of few words, but his food
speaks volumes. My 107 year old family business,
H.Forman & Son is the world's oldest producer of smoked
Scottish salmon, a product which used to be recognised
as one of the western world's most popular gourmet food,
but now is mostly mass produced by others. Through
Grant's passion and integrity he has never compromised
on product quality and despite commercial pressures he
has always remained loyal to our artisan and uniquely
hand-prepared methods, helping to maintain the true
traditions of this once great food. Grant deserves an
Olympic Gold medal!"
LANCE FOREMAN,

H. Forman & Son, London,
established 1905

Bohemian Pilsner, Melbourne

A Natural PASTURE FED
ANGUS steer carcase, sourced and processed by
the O'Connor family in Gippsland, southeast Victoria.
Recognized for its rich pastures and clean air and
water, Gippsland is Australia's most prized

BEEF producing region, and its most pristine
natural environment. The O'Connor family have been
supplying Natural, Hormone free beef from this region
for 3 generations We chose it's quality for Australian
Venues.

Hula show

Barley

"Sometimes it seems Grant's imaginative approach is to
walk through a black-and-white world and leave it in full
color.  For more than a decade I've seen him take an
ordinary food—a raisin, a pepper, a pistachio—and make
it beautiful in a hundred different ways."

JUDY HIRIGOYEN

Director, Global Marketing, American pistachio
growers association

"Grant is a great friend, business partner, father &
fearless ringleader. "Mac"Fasten your seatbelt.
I'm sure it'll be a great ride."

SAMMY D
AKA CHEF DEMARCO

8 pistachio nuts